Umbilical

POEMS

Michael Spence

WINNER OF THE NEW CRITERION POETRY PRIZE

St. Augustine's Press
SOUTH BEND, IN

Funding for this year's New Criterion Poetry Prize
has been provided by Joy & Michael Millette

www.staugustine.net

Library of Congress Cataloging-in-Publication Data is available.

ISBN: 978-1-58731-874-0

Umbilical

Also by Michael Spence:

The Bus Driver's Threnody

Crush Depth

Adam Chooses

The Spine

Contents

For my mother, Eileen M. Spence (1923–2001)

Acknowledgments

Grateful acknowledgment is made to the following publications in which many of these poems were first published.

Atlanta Review: "The Exhortation of the Pigeon God"
The Chariton Review: "Deep Crooked," "The Famous Writer Counseling Ben Brown," "Geedunk," "Kalgoorlie," "Pacifica," and "Talk Radio"
Ekleksographia: "Elegy for the One-Hundred-Year-Old Fir"
The Gettysburg Review: "Rottnest Island"
The Hurricane Review: "Ars Prosetica"
Literary Imagination: "Avocettina" and "Oppidum"
Measure: "The Walna Scar Road"
The New Criterion: "Combined Campaign," "His Reason," and "Umbilical"
The New York Quarterly: "Hunting Game"
The North American Review: "Downpour" and "The Edge of Fall"
Notre Dame Review: "New River"
The Seattle Review: "Glacier National Park, Montana"
The Sewanee Review: "Rationing the War," "'We Can Do It!,'" and "When Those at Home First See" (first published in Vol. CXVIII, No. 2, Spring 2010)
Sewanee Theological Review: "Homecoming"
Shenandoah: "Plutonium—Its Root"
Southern Humanities Review: "Modern Sculpture"
Tampa Review: "Lament for Roral, Roric, Rorid, and Rory"
Tar River Poetry: "A Brown Study," "Mortar," and "Ten Nickels: New Orleans, 1965"
The Yale Review: "Broken Sonnet: Divorce" and "My Mother's Last Christmas Card, Unsent"
"The Long Life of Death" and "Way Station" reprinted by permission from *The Hudson Review*, Vol. LXVIII, No. 2 (Summer 2015). Copyright © 2015 by Michael Spence.

"Aubade: Elegy for the Sun," "Hunting Game," and "Umbilical" were reprinted in *Floating Bridge Review*, Number Six, 2013.

"My Mother's Last Christmas Card, Unsent," was reprinted in *Limbs of the Pine, Peaks of the Range*, David D. Horowitz, ed., (Rose Alley Press, 2007).

"Broken Sonnet: Divorce," "Pacifica," and "Talk Radio" were reprinted in *Many Trails to the Summit*, David D. Horowitz, ed., (Rose Alley Press, 2010.)

"My Mother's Last Christmas Card, Unsent," was reprinted on the *Poetry Daily* website on October 14, 2004.

My thanks as always to my fellow members of the Decasyllables for their encouragement and sharp suggestions for making my work stronger: John Davis, Sharon Hashimoto, Susan Landgraf, Judy Lightfoot, Robert McNamara, Arlene Naganawa, Ann Spiers, and John Willson.

And special thanks to Jim Barnes, George Core, Jessica Faust, Vince Gotera, Mark Jarman, Luke Whisnant, and David Yezzi, who have given me their constant support over the years. They have helped to clear the twisting path I've taken since I first set foot on it.

Thanks also to Stonehouse (Miramonte, CA) and the Whiteley Center (Friday Harbor, WA) for granting me time and support to write some of these poems and organize this book.

My love to Sharon, who is my tether
These days we climb the hills together.

Umbilical

I. Motherlands

Oppidum

(Caesar's term for a hill-town lived in by Celts.)

In the Age of Iron, a man
Emerges from his hut.
He carries a metal bowl,
The sun polishing its curve
As he walks to a huge wall.

He helped his tribe to build
This rampart around their hill—
Blocks of unhewn stone
Without mortar, held in place
By their weight alone.

Erecting giant statues
To Mars, Rome calls
His people savage. Of the figures
Built to his gods, not one
Is taller than a man.

He sits and unwraps his tools.
Etching a filigree
Fine as web, his chisel
Carves the bowl: threads
Of light coil and fall.

A boy runs past, but stops
Before the man's hut. Edging
Closer, the child stares
Up at the dark niches
Carved above the door.

Then he laughs at what he sees.
The skulls of enemies
Grin down at him,
As though they hear his cries—
They also once had eyes.

Mortar

for Sharon, in the Lake District

The rock creases my hand
When I lean against these walls,
And I start to understand
Their builders. Hearing the call

Which pulls travelers up
Onto crests of broken stone
Where sky like an inverted cup
Rings their edge, those who own

These hills have made their gates
Without padlocks. They trust
That, when we enter, we'll wait
To close them as neighbors must.

Searching for sights, we tourists
Tramp high into fields
Growing only mists
And mud and bracken. Concealed

In the ferns, a sheep bleats
Half-heartedly; just
Enough to keep our feet
From wandering off the rust-

Colored gouge we climb.
These piled stones, their weight
Their only mortar, mime
A hedgerow of slate.

Embedded in the rock,
The worn slats of a stile
Gray as graphite squeak
When we step over. *A trial*

By muck, you joke. Most
Of the path uphill a mire,
We pass a Roman outpost
Fallen like its empire.

At last we reach the height
That isn't on our maps.
We see the builders' sight
Is clear, though fog wraps

The hilltops in a kind
Of web that holds sound:
Moving skyward binds
Us closer to the ground.

New River

(West Virginia)
for William Hoffman

The only river older is the Nile.
Walking a trail along the mountainside,
You watch the water: it seems to lie a mile
Below this steep slope. A storm froze a hide

Of ice to the trees. Their limbs bent and broken,
The shattered trunks of royal paulownias
Make you think of carvers in Japan
Who prize the wood—wood so fine that outlaws

Rustle the trees, floating them downriver.
At last you reach the Kaymoor mine, its rails
And water tanks, the iron on its wooden cars
Flaking to rust. Out beyond the tipple

Squat the coke ovens. Weeds festoon
Their crumbling faces. You rub their stone:
Pitted, reminding you of Aztec ruins.
Strange how the places closest to a man

Will give him thoughts of places far away.
But the land farthest from him is the past.
Your great-grandfather worked this mine. Each day
In a wagon hooked to a cable, braced

Against wind and sleet, the miners rode
Down to the bench-level, digging darkness
Out of the earth. New River flows the shade
Of coal, as though its waters still sluice

Their loads. The foreign land the miners found
Lies beneath your feet. Some lived their lives
                              underground
In that warm, endless night, and never knew
The waters in a river could run blue.

Rationing the War

A good thing I suffered through the Depression
Before I hit this.
After all I did without, I don't miss
What now takes coupons

To buy: any meat that isn't Spam,
Gasoline,
Rubber for my car's tires, seams of nylons
On girly gams.

Too old, recruiters told me. So I went home,
Forced to troll
For victory in my garden, digging little foxholes
For seeds in the loam.

But I hate when coffee and sugar disappear—
That makes it tough
To haul out of bed and weld the stuff
That jams up the gears

Of the Axis. Even the kids chip in:
Save the scraps,
Their hand-scrawled posters say, *to beat the Japs*.
We want to win

So bad, we look like mirrors: smiling to keep
Morale high
Till our faces ache. Some people can buy,
No matter how steep

The cost. Mister Black will find it for me
If I've got the pull.
He runs his market while pennies turn to steel,
And soldiers die for free.

Pacifica

We're warring with a land whose name
No one is sure how to pronounce.
Shot three times, my cousin comes home
On crutches. Yet I hardly glance

At the headlines: I know the walls
Of the university are airtight—
No draft can ever reach me. Still
I wonder: *Is what I'm doing right?*

Am I just afraid? My neighbors fear
The strangers they call Cong the way
"Natives" feared the giant ape. Here
The rain owns the sky for days,

Light blurring the edge of shadows
The madronas leak. When students burn
Their cards, our leaders—a new game show!—
Pull our birthdates from a drum: I learn

I'm "fifteen." The light at the tunnel's end
Become a fire, I join the navy—
A mammal that forsakes a land
Of flames by returning to the sea.

Avocettina

for Arlene Naganawa

Your name from a bird,
You are pre-bird: a long
Illuminated whip
Of sea creature, head
Vaguely avian.
To your depth, light
Does not reach. We bring
Our own so we can see you
Sharper than you see us. But
You truly are illuminated—
A strand of sun coiling
Far below the surface
Where the real sun floats
Its broken pieces, trying
To assemble an animal
As sinuous as you.
Harboring your narrow light,
You glide through a darkness
Of overwhelming pressure—
You with no need for wings.

Rottnest Island

Australia, 1990

Thinking the sandy flats
And scrub brush writhed with rats,
A Dutch explorer named
The island *rat nest*.
                            Who blamed
Him? How was he to know
The mammals digging burrows
Beneath his salt-stained soles
As he tramped among the boles
Of eucalyptus were not
The kind of vermin brought
Ashore by his own ship?

As these flowers weren't tulips:
The Rottnest daisy a weed,
The sandflower a breed
Of reddish rubber that clung
To slopes like flaking dung—

Although its blossom, small
And white, made him recall
Those chalices of paleness
Back home that would press
His window looking out
On the Zuider Zee.
                            No doubt
The quokkas, with rodent fur

And bald tails, became a blur
Of scurry at the distance
His crew saw them from. A glance
Around was all he need spare:
His reading of their spoor
Confirmed his first belief.
For naming things was a proof
Of his work,
                    and we make charts
By sketching in the parts
We know first. Though the hide
Feels soft, and quokkas abide
Men as do friendly pets,
They *are* rat-like.
                    Now, nets
Of orange plastic ring
The freshly planted saplings
To stop the teeth that would tear
Them dead.
                    An oil tanker
Has sunk here — the current unravels
The vessel. Fish nose the hull
Softly, turning its grief
Into shelter: an iron reef.

Ars Prosetica

I'd like to claim I came to poetry
Because the love of verse overwhelmed me.

Sure, in the sixth grade I memorized
"The Raven"—well, the first stanza. This disguised

In art my fascination with the dark
And strange. Every ocean held a shark

Back then. What else was all that water for
But to conceal a creature made of hunger?

The way they taught a poem in high school
Was as if it were some sort of puzzle:

The meaning trampled by the jackboot tread
Of the beat, hogtied in lines that knotted

My tongue whenever I had to "explicate."
Besides, who cared? I figured no one wrote

Poems any more. When Frost had died
In '63, that's what my teachers implied:

Verse had been commandeered by greeting cards,
And poetry hijacked by fuzzy bards

Like Rod McKuen who lapped their lonelymilk
In public. A real writer needed the bulk

And bite only prose allowed—this was clear.
Then a college prof read Kinnell's "The Bear"

Out loud: a hunt across a frozen sea;
A wounded beast; a man hungry

Enough to drink blood. When I felt wind
Sear my skin, my ears filled with the sound

Of howling, and I knew I had to trace
Its source. I stepped out onto that bauchy ice

To place my footprints in a world that grows
A rigid hide for the ocean coiling below.

Deep Crooked

The river where he wanders, twisted tight
As a poisoned cottonmouth, hides shadows
In its curves. Are they something more than skins
The night abandons? He watches mud creep up
Around his work boots—the sucking sound
Of letting go. A special bend, he thinks,
Where he stands now: a maple overhangs
The water, split at its base. Has he caught the tree
In the act of opening itself, or sealing?
Its cavity can hold whatever he'll place there
Later. Even in the widest clearing, sunlight
Falls on only half of him.

                                        Still
Waters, they called him when a child: he looked
So deeply into all he saw, down past
The husks which everyone around him called
The world, believed *enough*. Biology
He loved: the science taught him patience leads
To answers. Methodically dissecting frogs—
Cold creatures baptized in formaldehyde
(That puzzle word: what does the formal hide?)—
He started wondering. Did life cling
Like a limpet to the reef-rock of its host,
Or would it let go easily as seed pods
From a dandelion?

Were people any different?
Although he looked like them, he never felt
They were his kind. The place he'd lived so long
Till he could finally leave—the attic room,
Its floor of splinters, ceiling leaning down
Against his face as he huddled to sleep like a door
He had no key for. . . .

His first experiments
Outside of school—the drunk whose smell stung
Sharp as something pulled from another type
Of pickling jar, the wandering child neglected
By its mother where the park path veered
Into trees—these proved his thesis: pain removed
The carapace of language, leaving just
The animal cries.

Divided into parts,
The whole becomes less mysterious—
To separate the flesh from bone would show
Him the essential frame, the structure, and so
The reason for the need to hide it all.
To hide it from everyone but those whose eyes
Stayed open.

He doesn't know how many
He will need as he steps toward the maple.
The hole is large, its darkness calling him
To fill it with the bones. To tilt them together
Like a sort of shelter, or kindling for a fire.
Trembling, he rubs his hands. The wind stirs
As he moves closer, and the shadows waver,
Making room for him.

Pinkville: My Lai, March 16, 1968

We owned the day, they owned the night.
—popular saying among American GIs

Larry aimed his machine gun at the ground
As though he couldn't trust
The earth. The sound

Of his slowing rotors wound to silence, the dust
Like fog that he knew the light
Of morning would thrust

Aside. His chopper had set down at the site
Of a bunker: peasants hid
In its shadows. Cordite—

The war's perfume, he'd heard it called—slid
Across his sweating face.
His pilot, a kid

Like the approaching soldiers, climbed out to place
Himself between the squad
And the bunker. *In case*

This turns to shit, the pilot said, *if I nod,*
Bring your barrel up.
Doubt clawed

At Larry: weren't they here to guard the troops?
How could he open fire
On them? The group

Came to a halt behind their squad leader.
The pilot, a sergeant, shouted
At the officer,

You gotta give me time to get them out.
The lieutenant only laughed:
We'll get 'em out

With hand grenades. Larry felt a draft
Chill his hands as it blew
Through the ticking aircraft.

He watched the pilot. His grip on the gun grew
Slick when he heard him say,
My guns are on you.

Larry saw a soldier turn and look his way.
Slowly, he waved at the man.
A short delay—

Then the man waved back. The peasants ran
To the chopper, their only shield
His pilot. A plan

Too crazy to work, with all the people killed
So far: it looked like hundreds
Of bodies filled

The ditches. Larry rubbed his itching forehead—
Could they hold enough water
To dilute such red?

He was glad to finally see the rotors stir
The burning air and dust
The scene to a blur,

The bright morning blown away in the gust.
But when he dreams of that day,
It's always dusk.

Glacier National Park, Montana

Inside the gate I stop. What do I seek,
What catches my eye
When I walk into the gift shop and buy
The rattlesnake?

It comes the way we want the dangerous:
Gutted and skinned,
Cut into bite-size pieces and canned
In a sweet sauce.

But the meat still holds a wild flavor; the tongue
Wants to taste
All that the lips can't name. And travelers want most
To reach something

Not on their maps—a place they've never known.
The air grows cool
As we head up a highway the signs call
Going-to-the-Sun.

We feel a magnetism pulling us
That needles can't,
And we follow where it leads—to the points
On a tilted compass.

We watch water seeping steadily through cracks
In the Weeping Wall.
The time I carry on my wrist is too small
To break such rock,

Just as the word *park* could never contain
The ice on the peaks
That carved the valleys below. The glaciers make
A separate nation.

The Walna Scar Road

England, 1997

It's more a scar
Than a road: a car

Runs out of blacktop
Half a mile up

The first incline.
We hike toward the mine

Where they excavate
Coniston slate.

Streaked like marble,
The stone is dull

Green—the color
Of American dollars—

Which lends a facade
Of grace to a broad

Range of banks.
I grab a chunk,

But it's too big,
Making my pack sag;

So I take a splinter
For a souvenir.

We climb a path
That takes our breath

As much from the heat
And placing our feet

On cracked and loose
Stones as from views

Of these crags. A flock
Of sheep like rocks

Growing fleece
Instead of moss

Won't move as we pass
Near by. The grass,

Though short and flat
As a welcome mat,

Is abundantly crowned
With dung: the ground

Looks as if a sack
Of marbles black

And glistening was poured
Along the borders

Of this trail. The slant
Steepens, and we pant

Louder—the only speech
Now in our reach.

A walking tour,
Said the brochure

Convincing us to take
This trip through the Lake

District. Sweat
Itches its wet

Course down my neck
As if called by the beck

Whose dry bed
We must cross. Our tread

Becomes slow;
The way grows

More broken—we pause
To honor the laws

Of gravity.
Hoping to see

Its peak around
Each new bend

For so long,
We think we're wrong

When we reach the crest
Of this road at last.

Two thousand feet
In the air, we shout

Our triumph and tightly
Embrace. I recite

"The World is Too Much
With Us." Then we catch

Sight of a girl tossing
A pink plastic ring

For her dog. There's no pack
Or gear on her back—

She hiked all this way
Up just to play.

She waves as we begin
The long path down.

Way Station

Only a couple of people have been killed
At the transit center where I catch my bus.
That's not counting the one who jumped from the top
Of the parking garage. Or the wheelchair man
Beaten by that gang—he didn't die.

I need to put these things out of my mind.
I never learned to drive: I thought I'd have
My husband a lot longer. I can't forget
Completely—you have to stay alert. I heard
Another rider say this place is haunted.

It makes me imagine ghosts are circling
The station to shroud us with their white,
To erase us the way they've been erased. It scares me
To think like this. But for now, I'll have to wrap
The fear inside myself—here comes my bus.

The Paramilitaries' Final Act

They disappear so many citizens
Into the murk
Beyond the city's limits—like the work
Of dark magicians—

The town itself starts to vanish. Walls
Turn thin
As paper confessions. Doors begin
To crack and fall

At the knock of doubt: key to all dissolving.
After words
And gestures end, the boundaries are conjured
Away. The ring

Of sorcerers alone remains on stage.
Behind the stone
Of what used to be, the dwindling crowd is shown
A jungle rage.

Combined Campaign

The captain told us charity began
        Aboard his aircraft carrier: the place
We had to call home. *We're in a race*
        With all the others—when we get every man

To voluntarily contribute, we'll win
        The plaque for Most Generous Ship in the Fleet!
Department heads like mine would repeat
        This lofty goal at every briefing to ensigns

Like me: we had to raise the largest pile
        And put the Old Man on its top. Like a prayer
I kept reciting, I urged my men to care
        For "all of those less fortunate"—the smile

I gave them felt sincere. As we got close
        To complete compliance (Comp-Comp), the
                        mood
Grew buoyant as a following sea. Then rude
        As a reef on no one's chart, a sailor said *no.*

A sailor in my division. Seaman Ames
        Told me he didn't believe in charity:
We gotta help ourselves up, don't we?
        That's what it says in the Bible. Back home,

They say begging breaks a man like a dry stick.
He looked like one himself—tall and thin,
Stiff as he sat in my office. I tried to pin
The "teamwork" ribbon on him; I tried the
gimmick

Of saying this could hurt his career. He blinked
At that: *I thought they said United Way*
Was voluntary. You're gunna force me to pay?
I told my boss, the First Lieutenant. His face
pinked

Down to the silver oak leaf on his collar.
What's wrong, ensign? Can't you motivate
Your own men? Try again and make him donate
His fair share. It's only a few dollars,

For Christ's sake. But Ames refused once more.
I'm only one guy—what's the big deal? I want
Them all to leave me alone. He looked more gaunt
Than he had the last time; he said other sailors

Were screwing with him about this Combined Campaign.
I'm so pissed off, I'll never give a thing
To it now! I told the First Lieutenant, who hung
His head and said to his blotter's coffee stains:

Did the iron fist in your velvet glove just turn
      To rust? He waved me away without looking up.
When the Donors' List was posted, I saw the ship
      Had reached Comp-Comp. That day I went
                                             astern

And found Ames leaning on the taffrail,
      Spitting into our wake. I asked what made
Him change his mind. *The First Lieutenant paid*
      For me! He scowled and stood straight as a nail:

Take my name off that list! It makes me look
      Like I broke! I said I'd see, but we both knew
We'd lost. On the hangar deck, they mustered the crew
      To applaud the captain as he raised his plaque.

II. Mother Tongues

Plutonium—Its Root

elegy for Rocky Flats

Plutonium—its root
Burrows down to the lord
Of the underworld.

Below the surface, they dug
For the base metal they turned
Into the triggers.

They said the more we had,
The more we wouldn't have
To use them.

The peace we'd known could end
Tomorrow. They said this
For fifty years.

They said an enemy
Far away lay waiting
To harm our children.

Rocky Flats lies
Close to Denver. They said
There was no danger.

Near the plant, a farmer
Held a dead chick,
Its bills twisted.

His children dug in the sand,
Singing the song we sang—
What we can't see

Can't hurt. Something
In the milk they drank still makes
A needle jump.

Broken Sonnet: Divorce

I never knew the birds
The way she did—
To me, a cormorant appeared
To be an egret who shed
All his colors for black.
I forget if herons
Will mate for life. Do the males flock,
Or do they fly alone?
I need to find the name
Of one who leaves the land behind,
Making flight his home.
The wind
Will choose which feathers line a nest
And which glide into mist.

When Those at Home First See

Nearly two years pass
After Pearl was bombed
Before we're allowed to see
A photo of our dead.
And even this is late:
The three soldiers half-
Buried in the sand
As if unsure—to hide
Or be revealed?
Breakers rock and smooth
The beach. Men surface
Like starfish washed ashore
By some turmoil undersea.
Irregularities.
The dead lie as though holding
The ground more tightly,
Since it has lost its hold
On them. Or has the tide
Halted their burial
With its *now-I-come*
And *now-I-leave*, forever
Leaving them in this seam
Between the sand and water?
And still we see no faces—
Just the fabric of uniforms
Wet with dark, then drying.
This leaves us to imagine
The ones we love or the ones
We think are nameless. Palm up,

The arm that lies extended
Neither points nor grasps
But does not let us go.

Legend

Among the dozen
Beasts that wander
The Chinese calendar,
The dragon alone
No longer treads
The crags or wades
The bogs of earth; the air
Does not stir
With those clacking
Scythes of wings.
Maidens once afraid
Have married.
Where has it gone,
That fierce reptilian
Flame? I long
For the burning tongue
Across my skin—its rasp
My shivering. Wind grasps
Vainly for those wails
In the night. The stars
Are not the glitter
Of scales.

Downpour

for Robert Wallace (1932–1999)

No one but him
seeing the rain
start . . .
    — "Swimmer in the Rain"

The rain falls hard all day as if to press
The land flat beneath the splintering glass
Of its hammer—to bring everything low.
Today I hear you're gone. Outside, a willow
Blurs into strands of seaweed, and the egret
In your poem rises white and dripping. A net
Of bright static woven by the downpour
Collects the reeds and musseled pier. The shore
Is slowly left behind by the man who swims
As steady as the tide, stitching a seam
Between the air and water. You never said
Where he was bound. You sent him on ahead
To find the place your hands have shaped from rain—
The place you've gone, fleshed in its clear skin.

Lament for Roral, Roric, Rorid, and Rory

My dictionary states you're obsolete.
But each of you receives a separate entry
Which is identical: an adjective
Meaning *dewy*. In what past could people tell

The difference between the thin skin of wet
That sheathes the blades of grass at dawn, and its sea
Of sparking tips? Between what films the leaves
Of the madrona, and what beads will fall

From their lips? How much moisture forms the floats
In the fisher's net of a spider web? Who could see
How much it takes to lick the rocks alive
With lichen? Something made such eyes grow dull

Or the light brighten beyond this sight. Now shoots
Of grass hold only dew. No plea
Can bring you back. *Roral* will not lave
The tongues that don't recall they long for its growl.

Talk Radio

You can't blame me: I used to slam the rich
And mighty. The masses would not rise. A jock
Who worked FM part-time playing rock
And jazz for nickels to a shrinking niche
Of humble listeners, I changed my pitch
To reach the whole cathedral. Now the flock
That hears my organ swelling as I hawk
Belligerence and baby food can't switch
The station of the cross they're hung upon.
My belly is their compass, and my tongue
The needle weaving airwaves into gold:
The shade in which their paradise is drawn.
Like wire, my disembodied voice has strung
Their loose beads into a rosary I hold.

The Exhortation of the Pigeon God

for Sati Mookherjee

My children of the window ledge,
My speckled acolytes who wedge
Together in the cold like beads
On a rosary, who grip the heads
Of statues that you decorate
With bright toupees and epaulettes
Of chalk, fear not: for I am come
To deliver you from the meager crumbs
Of stale croissants and bagels strewn
Across the walk like sodden runes
By idle humans, from the curse
Of the mass who kick at you or worse,
Harass you with their dogs and cats,
Condemning you as "flying rats"—
I am come to tell you: Their day
Is over; for, of all the grays
Which claim their city, you are the one
That flies. Now take to air, my children—
The beat of your wings is the praise
That I must hear. O fill my gaze,
My flock, darkening the blue,
Chanting as you rise: *Coup! Coup!*

Hunting Game

My father never talked the way I will—
Maybe he thought the fewer words you use,
The more they mean. So Mom would have to tell
Me what he'd done. To be one of the guys,
He went with her cousins once to hunt deer.
They tramped through brush and crouched in the rain;
At night they swapped blue jokes and guzzled beer.
Well, the others did—sipping one can
Till it went flat, Dad stayed quiet. When at last
They shot a buck, he quit for good: *A gun
Is too real*, he later told her, *for just
A game*. So the time we fled a hurricane,
He took a pistol. Like him, it wouldn't speak
Unless we met a silence he'd have to break.

The Long Life of Death

We finally hear the news we've been praying for
On August fifteenth, 1945—
Japan's surrendered. *It's the end of the war,*
The guy beside me bellows: *We're still alive!*

Shooting and scrambling all over the rock
Of Okinawa for so long it seems
We were born doing it, at first we're in shock:
Is this a rumor? Some Tojo trick? But the screams

Of joy are spreading like flames through the palm fronds.
We're going home at last. Why did God spare
The men around me? We'll have a life beyond
All this. Yelling, we fire our guns into the air.

The shouts of celebration turn to cries
Of surprise and pain: GIs are spouting red,
Twisting, falling. Seven of us die
As the bullets rain back down on our heads.

Tic Didactic: After Reading Poems in *The Progressive*

Is it a poem if it's just the truth?
The truth's a lot, it's true—a glinting tooth
That punctures all the balloons swollen
By the stale exhaust of businessmen who've stolen
The public park to build their empty house.

Yes, freedom's a flame our leaders like to douse,
And who'd deny the rich are often callous
Though their hands and tongues are smooth and soft?
                                        The palace
Of the CEO is what grows best in fields
Harrowed of their farmers.

                        But facts should yield
More than bite marks to be art. Instead
Of sincerity's astringent wine, some bread
For a meal. To hint the tyrant's winter will break,
A fang of sunlight lies on a frozen lake.

The Famous Writer Counseling Ben Brown

Career? Forget it; everything will come
In its own time,
Intoned the guy who'd won two Guggenheims,
Whose seven volumes

Of poetry were published by Knopf,
Whose work that week
Appeared in The New Yorker and The Atlantic.
You're better off

Not thinking of awards or publications;
For writing poems,
The man said, smiling like a garden gnome,
Is a vocation,

Not a business. His Oxfords squealing high
As a laugh when he turned,
He left his listener in the hall. I've learned,
Thought Brown with a sigh,

I'll get nowhere with a commercial house;
I can't charm
Even the "literary" (their names like law firms'—
Farrar, Straus,

& Giroux; Harcourt Brace Jovanovich);
I've given up
On college presses like LSU; there's no hope
I'll be jerked awake

By a Lannan or MacArthur phone call.
I never dreamed
I'd scale those blinding peaks. But I *had* aimed
At the foothills.

What more do I drop to make me pure enough?
How low do I set
My sights? Looking down, he knew: Till I shoot
My work boots off.

Exhibition

Administrators fear this penis: red
And blunt as brick, gripping with a growl
The barbell in its teeth. What sort of head
Envisions this? Like catchers after foul
Balls, they scramble to snatch from others' sight
This thing whose sting squints their eyes.
        The artist—
Prophet? jester?—does he mean to indict
The tribe of males who, raising iron, insist
The more they grunt, the more they get it up?
Or how hard it is to be a man? How hard
A man must be?
     To blur the world in syrup
So all will swallow, the veiling ones guard
Us from a life that's something to anoint
With a horizontal exclamation point.

Geedunk

The word plugs my ear when I wake: *Geedunk*
(Pronouncing it evokes the sound of a rock
Dropped in mud) is Navyese for junk-
Food. *So what?* I think, till a crying flock

Of gulls reminds me I'm on the ship, my home
Away from homeland, where the lonely pair
Of vices authorized for killing time
On watch are cigarettes and coffee. *Beware*

Addiction, my ensign brain advises my mouth;
You might become a lifer. I feel proud
Of my willpower when I later pass the uncouth
Blob of a senior officer who crowds

The open hatchway to the weatherdeck
Like Justice missing the blindfold: the balance
Trays of his hands hold a mug and a smoke.
I grin, ascending to my stateroom. A glance

In the mirror—what's that smear on my cheek?
Chocolate. Wiping it off, I reach far
Back in my desk safe to the jumbo box
And wriggle out another Snickers bar.

Catechism

It's on again: the dragon dark and fierce
As a cartoon can be on 1950's TV.
"Baker's Instant" (intoned by voices deep
And manly), followed by four beats
On a bass drum—*Dum da dum-dum!*
A mounted knight with lance charges forth,
Strikes: an explosion of scales
That scatter like confetti—as if the beast
Is hollow as a pinata. Thus the knight ends
My night: I shiver, knowing I'll awake
To Sister Morgan's catechism class.
The "Love Divine" which Father Dunn proclaims
Is left behind when Mass comes to a close;
With his final blessing, we children clomp
Down to the basement. Its heat is turned too high,
And dampness from our coats and shoes rises
Like souls of steam. Sister Morgan, thin
As though compressed between two giant hands,
Points to a ring of folding chairs that squeak
As they bear our weight. She slowly grins. *Hell*
Lies all around us, she declares; *you kids*
Are just too young to see it yet. The boy
Beside me mispronounces: *kittychasm.*
Her smile doesn't reach her eyes—I think of cats
Thrown into a flaming valley. *God*
Will burn you up, she squints, leveling an arm
Straight as a lance at the boy. Every Sunday,
She details how the world I've barely arrived in
Is over. Her wimple like a raised visor,

She tells us, *Satan can claim anyone*:
You all must pray for mercy. So I pray
Saturday will have no end, the knight
On horseback never reach the dragon. I hear
What Sister Morgan sees: the Devil's fire
Ignites the tinder which we least suspect
Till all is conflagration. Her eyes gleam
Like the flame that hollows out the votive candles.

The Tower

after a print by M. C. Escher

Black and white, the colors
Of the builders and their world;
Black the edges of the blocks
Of white stone, black
The ground and the rooftops
Of buildings far below.
Those buildings, blunt as the blocks
That make the tower, build
A city by the sea. The water
Shines like bands of heat.
When matter ascends from solid
To liquid, the light touching it
Comes away brighter.
The viewer floats like God
Above the tower: the men on top
Greater than it. Matter striving
To reach the light of heaven,
They expand like fish released
From the pressure of great depths.
Wandering the earth, those below
Are small, aimless as fish eggs.
The builders head ever upward,
Gaining size and shape
From their direction. At the top,
A man extends his black arms,
Ready to rise to the sun.

The gesture signs to God his question:
Where is the end of the sky?

The Edge of Fall

We claimed that we were Number One,
So in New York, we said it twice:
The towers thrust into the skies
Like a Roman numeral two. The sun
Touched them first like a light on a stage.
But others saw the bars that stripe
A dollar sign. This morning wipes
The buildings from the day's blue page.
Now, we see the towers rise again
Through their ghosts, dark and straight,
Engraving this September date
In Arabic: eleven.

III. Blood Mothers

Umbilical

for my mother

Not flesh but string, the line which bound your foot
To mine, hobbling me so you could nap
And not worry I would wander loose
Those summer afternoons. But who could sleep
In such light? No boy of eight. I'd wait
Until your breath grew even. Holding mine,
I'd sit up slowly, carefully work the knot—
A ball of snake coils small but intricate
As trip-wires. One day I slipped the noose,
Eased off the creaking bed. I felt my face
Tighten around the eyes. Afraid you'd call
Me back, I tiptoed toward the doorway: no sign
I'd wakened you. I listened, then took a step
Through—and saw the darkness of the long hall.

"We Can Do It!"

slogan from World War II poster

I was brought up to believe in bringing up
Children: that was the most important job
I could have. Getting married, having kids—
Like breathing in and breathing out. The war
Changed my mind; I was riveted
By the story of Rosie rolling up her sleeve
And flexing her muscle the way my husband did
When we were courting. He had been the one
To fix the broken washer and keep the car
Running "smooth as castor oil," he'd joke.

When he and most the other men sailed off,
I learned to repair airplane accessories—
Starters, generators, alternators. Me!
Who never even went to high school.
I walked down rows of Plexiglas noses
For B-17 bombers, polishing them
Until they gleamed like see-through igloos.
Even for a woman, I was small—
A bare five feet in my bare feet.
So I would grab a flashlight and crawl
Up into the gas tanks to look for leaks.
I felt like I was part of something larger
Than myself, my little goals and worries.
And money: I'd never made so much. I bought
The kinds of food I'd always dreamed of—steak,
Not hamburger. And ice cream by the gallon.

Sometimes I'd share it with the other gals
At the plant, but not always. Heck, they could buy
Their own.

    The men of course would cluster around us
Thick as seeds on a dandelion. Pretty
Wasn't part of it—the homeliest could get
A hometown hero. I never told my husband
All that I did. And he was smart enough,
When he got back, not to ask. He never told
Me everything that happened overseas.
These days, our life and love are quiet ones.
I help him change the transmission or rebuild
The carburetor. As he lies beneath the car,
I can hand him any tool he can name.

Modern Sculpture

for Henry Moore

The vertebrae, bronze
And stark, could be the jacks
In a child's game. But their size:

A kid who played with these
Would loom as large as the bank
Whose doors they lie before,

All his body growing
But his mind. Three figures
In a row—monument

To a new god; trinity
Of an age that gnaws everything
To bone. Verdigris

Rubs their hollows, leaving
A dust the shade of money
On brass knuckles.

A Brown Study

I have been half in love
            with easeful Death . . .
—Keats, "Ode to a Nightingale"

And now the other half embraces it,
Brown thinks, re-reading his rejection letter:
"Your poems could bore a stone to dust." He tears
The corners from the paper, lets them flit
Like ragged snowflakes to the midnight blue
Linoleum. He tears some more—a blizzard
Slow and sparse, its howling only heard
By him. Brown blinks: *This is what I do—*
I tear off pieces of myself to set
Against some darkness that will make them glow.
The paper flecks are stars: a scattering
Of days when his life had flared. He'd tried to string
A constellation from their tattered net
To hold his name. He leans down, and blows.

Ten Nickels: New Orleans, 1962

for my mother

We stare as our bluejeans chase
Themselves inside the dryer
Like skins from the life we erase
Each time we move. The whir

Of the laundromat, the heat
And damp swelling the air
Make me twitch in my seat.
Seattle didn't prepare

Us for the wilting drive
Through summer to New Orleans.
Though you swear no one can live
Here and not go insane,

You press your lips tight
To keep from telling Dad.
Designing rockets for flights
To the moon means he had

To take the transfer, to "follow
The contrail" wherever it led.
I say I want to go—
I'm tired, and my head

Is dizzy as the laundry
Spinning around; I whine
I want to watch TV
At the motel. (Its sign

Buzzes like flies all day
Outside the cramped room
Where our family has to stay
Till Dad finds us a home.)

You tell me to hush and act
Like your oldest son should.
Using a paperback
As a fan, you sigh, *Be good*.

But I only complain more.
I'll bet you fifty cents,
You say with a weary glare,
You can't keep silent

For a whole ten minutes.
Can too; I pretend to lock
My lips as I calculate—
Five *Flash* comic books

Could be mine, or a batch
Of Butterfingers. You warn,
Not a peep; just watch
The clock. My tongue burns

In the oven of my mouth.
I wipe my face on the shoulder
Of my teeshirt. In this steambath,
I dream I'm underwater:

The clock's a pressure gauge
On a sub. Words clog my throat.
Even time can't dodge
This heat, which knocks it out.

At last you count out nickels
As the dryer, ceasing to hum,
Stops. The small pile
Clinks like ice in my palm.

Kalgoorlie

Australia, 1990

This sand is red as skin
Burned by the sun—searing
Like the spark of a lit fuse—that hisses
Up into a sky grown pale
As skin once was.

The red seeps into the brickwork
Of the church, into the paint
On the cinderblock whorehouse:
Each building a complementary half of the other world
The miners need.

The girders and iron walkways
Of the Mount Charlotte Mine, flecked
With rust dark as dried blood, reach out
Like a net of metal nerves
With its flesh burned off.

A hundred thousand tons of ore are pulverized
Every year. Its grade is poor:
Eight tons dissolve in the acid
Made from miners' sweat to yield a single ounce
Of gold.

On Croesus Street, named for a king so wealthy
That people shivered, stands an office
Bleached colorless. Inside it labor the Little Sisters

Of the Poor. The heat
Makes its edges ripple like small flames.

C. Y. O'Connor sweated to devise a scheme
To bring water here—the townsfolk laughed
Until he killed himself. His bust
Now rests in the park, surrounded by the water
Of a pond.

The townsfolk planted a eucalyptus
Where gold was first found. They've had to replace the
                                                    tree
Five times: the dogs, narrowing
Their red eyes,
Keep digging till it falls.

Homecoming

for Susan Landgraf

The story's told: too many
Martians and not enough spaceships
to take them back . . .
—"Why Some Hungarians Dream Notes or Numbers," S. L.

Watching the portal iris open, they see
Red has always been their favorite color.
This desert makes them understand the flag
Of Hungary—three bars, red over white
Over green: Mars over Earth. From the rust edge
Of the horizon, a canal stretches toward them
Like an empty vein searching for new blood.
It's only right that they should be first
To step out on this sand—their Mother
Of Millennia strode these dunes long before

Their ancestors came to Earth. But a ship
Of that fleet exploded; the stranded were forced
To hide. Finding the native blood was red,
They mixed with it: a perfect camouflage.
Harder to hide the ancient tongues—its rhythms
Flowed strong; they saw its symbols in the dark
Connecting the stars. Their children touched
Their past by writing songs and solving equations:
What Earth knew as music or numbers, they heard
As equal halves which joined to make their words.

Under a sun hot and swollen, they acted
Human. But their faces at night lifted
To the sky. They longed to feel the wind of home
That kept the dunes always moving. Love
Of notes and figures combined in their offspring
With love for the green world: when the time came,
Many would not board the craft. But the rest
Were drawn like blood returning to the heart.
As they climb the first red swell, they hear
Again the music of another sphere.

Her Arms

I.

My mother pulled her blouse sleeve up and flexed—
Whatcha think? she asked me. *Pretty good*
For a lady, huh? Her biceps like a lump

In plaster seemed to make the skin gleam
With tension. She smiled: *I got this chopping wood*
As a girl. It looked about the same as mine.

Swinging that ax also gave me this.
Pressing fingertips against her palm,
She bent that fist forward—a knot of tendons

Bunched beneath her wrist. *Wanna test*
My grip? Fourteen, already taller than her,
I said okay. We'd never shaken hands.

Her fingers warm and firm, she hung on tight.
I met her steady pressure with my own.
She grinned: *Can't you squeeze any harder?*

Uncertain of the look she gave me, I nodded.
Then do it. I bore down more; her eyes
Widened, a chirp of pain escaping her.

I let loose as though electrocuted—
I asked if I had hurt her. Her left hand
Reached to rub her palm, then stopped.

Of course not. She laughed: *I guess you're strong*
Enough. Then she patted my shoulder. *Some day,*
We'll have to see how well you can chop wood.

2.

That's when I first really saw—just below
Her wrist—the small tattoo: a dagger.
A simple outline drawn and filled with blue

Darker than her veins, over her pulse,
It looked more like a birthmark. When I pointed,
She smiled: *My mother and I exchanged words*

When I came home that day and showed her. She turned
Her hand to examine the sliver shape. I asked
If it hurt. *Like I'd been branded. But I denied*

I felt a thing. Mother'd told me the world
Was a hard place—when my dad died, I learned
You need a tough hide. She rubbed the mark

As if to press it deeper into her.
Funny: your dad was in the navy in the war,
But who's the one who got tattooed?

3.

Blurred dagger, stiletto silhouette—
When did you arise from the thin skin
Of her wrist to take on edge and weight?

Each time when Dad got transferred for his job,
He'd leave ahead of us like an explorer
To clear the path and make our journey safe.

He should have carried a Bowie knife to blaze
The unknown trees, I thought as a kid, or fight off
Beasts that lurked to leap out from them.

But that day I helped my mother make their bed,
I grabbed a pillow and heard something thunk
The floor. A leather sheath holding a knife

Lay by my toes. I picked it up. *That's mine,*
She said, her hand outstretched. She held it close.
For protection till your father's back.

Blurred dagger, stiletto silhouette—
Like something from inside her that she needed.
I helped her put the covers back in place.

Something Solid

for my cousin, Phil

My mother held the snub-nose .38
Her brother Jack had given her: *On loan,*
He said, *to keep you safe.* She felt a weight
Dense enough to sink into the bones

Of her hand. Despite her knife, she told my uncle,
While Dad was away, she wanted *something solid.*
The metal turned the light that struck it dull,
As though avoiding notice was how a weapon did

Its worst damage. But the bullets drew her eye:
Brass and lead like identical slugs to typeset
A language of one word. The night Jack died,
Phil came over to our house to get

His father's gun back. Seeing the furrows
Scar his brow like Jack's wasn't enough
For Mom. She touched his face: *Just let me know
If you ever need me to knock someone off.*

My Name

For years, I hated the name
My father gave me: *Spence*—
Rhyming with *fence, nonsense,*
And *dense*. It was to blame

For the smart-ass limerick
That kid in junior high
Singsonged about me. Try
To say it: no trick

The tongue or mouth may know
Can prevent having to hiss
A moment while you press
Your lips together as though

Pronouncing the word *spit*.
How could any boy
With a name like that enjoy
The respect of pals? To quit

Thinking of it, I'd pretend
My surname was *Bannon*.
This word boomed like *cannon*,
Something my few friends

Would envy. The "Johnny Quest"
Cartoon on TV had
The answer. Johnny's dad,
A scientist, relied on the best

Sidekick ever. "Race"
Bannon, with his deep suntan
And voice: the kind of man
Who could fly jets, face

Danger every week—
A space monster or horde
Of skeletons with swords—
And never grow weak

With fear. (And *his* was the name
My mother had had before
She married my father.) I swore
I'd avoid the life of shame

Which lay in wait, and shuck
The word like an empty rind.
This year in England, I find
My name by merest luck

On a wooden map that shows
A country branching with names—
Every square inch claims
A dozen as kin. Below

Spence, it lists this blithe
Origin: though a word
The rub of time has blurred,
Its root seems to be *scythe*.

An engineer, my father
Never had a sidekick
And didn't believe in quick
Solutions. He wouldn't bother

To explain—doing his work,
He would whispershear
The tangled grass, trying to clear
My path with every arc.

The Muse Descends on Ben Brown

Can't you see I'm busy? shouted Brown,
Wishing that he were. He quickly grabbed
The pen abandoned on the pad and frowned
To show his concentration. Leaning, she dabbed

At her reflection in his whiskey glass.
So many facets, she sighed, *to a narrow vision.*
Then she saw his doodles. *Trying to pass
For a cartoonist now?* She snickered. *None*

Of these will get you syndicated. Crumpling
The sheet, he bellowed, *What kind of muse are you,
Huh? You're supposed to help my words take wing!
But every time you come here, you pour glue*

In my inkwell! She tossed her frosted hair
And laughed: *You use a ballpoint.* He threw the Bic
At her; it passed right through and struck a chair.
That won't help, she giggled. *Now answer me quick—*

You want to make it big? He filled his glass: *Be thrilled
To make it medium.* She tapped her fingertips
Together; a tinkling like wind chimes spilled
From her glittering nails. *That's why I made this trip,*

She grinned. *I realized we've had the cart
Before the jackass. Your being famous* first
Is the most important part of pushing your art.
Ben stared at her, his jaw slack, then cursed:

Are you insane? Who the hell ever heard
Of a writer being praised before he wrote?
The Muse grew angry, or his vision blurred—
Around her, darkness shimmered like a moat

Guarding an alabaster castle. *Look,*
She spat. *You know how many movie stars*
And presidents and stuff have gotten books
Of poems published? The line would stretch to Mars!

Ben took a belt: *That's where their crap belongs.*
The Muse chortled—*You mean on all those shelves*
In bookstores? People want the kind of songs
They can whistle. Let's quit fooling ourselves.

She stroked his cheek. *At least you could cultivate*
Some becoming eccentricities: shave
One side of your face, or—this *would be great*—
Stand in a garbage can and do The Wave

When you read! Brown sagged—*And light my ass on fire*
With my pages, too. Then that's where my *work*
Would belong. She lifted his chin. *You never tire*
Of dramatizing, do you? I'm going berserk

Trying to force-start your career! I've lost
The other Muses' respect—though I tell them, "What kind
Of splash can anyone expect when you've tossed
Such a small stone into the well?" So find

Your niche, Ben—she pinched his ear—*before*
The only one left open is your grave.
Near tears, from either sorrow or his sore
Ear, Ben begged, *Give me some advice! Save*

Me! She let go his lobe. *Something short*
Will sell—*and sexy. Hmm . . . here's what you do*—
She poked his beer gut and said with a snort—
Write me a book of obscene haiku!

Elegy for the One-Hundred-Year-Old Douglas Fir

Was this your slow-motion revenge
Against the house that spelled your death?
The builders must have severed your roots.
He checks the snapshot: needles, green
Two years ago, now grown brown
As though you'd turned deciduous;
Limbs twisted and hanging like deadfalls
Waiting for a signal; the sap
That streaked your cracking trunk with a drool
Gold and hard. And always the wind
Making you creak and lean toward his home.
Despite his wish, he calls the cutters.
The chainsaws only halt their whine
When another chunk of you—huge
As a wine cask for the gods—lets go.
With each impact, he feels the shudder
Through his feet like a private earthquake:
As if this ground wants to leave with you.
When the noise and shaking stop, he finds
Too much blue spreads overhead.
The height above your stump is crowded
With the smell of resin. He leans down
To gaze into your warped bull's-eye,
Ripples frozen in your well.

Aubade: Elegy for the Sun

Ages back the sun
Began to swell, boiling
Our atmosphere away,
Casting into space
The numberless lives
Of all that lived.
This final dawn, no one
Is here—not the furthest
Grandchild we can dream of.
Growing beyond Venus,
The star swallows our world,
The vanished air replaced
By fire. This sunset will burn
For eons: a solo
Of last light; the red glow
We swam in before birth.

His Reason

What reason could a boy have to twist
The handle of hot all the way open,
Plunge his hands into the sink, palms

Pressed flat against the bottom?
To feel his skin electrified?
The pain stunning him motionless?

To keep his hands there till the boiling
Fogs his face in the mirror? To make his hands
Obey, to make them stay precisely

Where they're telling him so loudly they shouldn't be?
To defy his mother, the one now shouting:
My God, what are you doing? Letting her

Pull him free? The cooling as she rubs
His hands with cream? The hands he holds
Before her, red and new, stinging in the air.

My Mother's Last Christmas Card, Unsent

Dear Ruth & Bill,
                           So glad to hear you'll stay
At home this year—I find the celebrations
Get gaudier each season. Lord, the way
Some people light their houses. We're told to ration
Electricity . . . and by TV, yet! Sure—
With all this crazy blinking like the rides
At Coney Island back when we were poor
And happy. Three of my four kids cried
On that ferris wheel: which of them was brave?
(This pen's begun to skip—I need to bear
Down hard to get the letters out.) I gave
My shamrock necklace back to Ree to wear—
The jade's too green for me. Take care.
                           Love, Eileen
P.S. don't think I'll use this pen again

Downman Road: New Orleans, 1965

The place we lived is only water now.
Seattle couldn't steel us for that heat
And damp, the road tar sucking at our feet
As if to trap our family. Mom didn't know how
To avoid my father's transfer. *But I won't bow*
Like a wilting rhododendron; we're elite—
You kids remember that, she said, *when you eat*
Red beans and rice at school. She wouldn't allow
Us to talk like the locals. *Only a sloppy tongue*
Says "I never did him nothin'." They sound like clowns
Or morons. That mushy Creole's barely English—
Their brains must melt here. Dad climbing these rungs
For his job, she thought, had made us all step down
To live in this swamp, her lips pressed thin as her wish.

To live in this swamp, her lips pressed thin as her wish
To go home to the Northwest, she had to shield
Her skin from the steeper sun, the way she concealed
From us her words with Dad. To admit a blemish
On face or marriage would be wrong as seeing fish
Appear on the front lawn. How it appealed
To her sense of sarcasm that "Elysian Fields"
Was the name of a nearby neighborhood. *They banish*
Us to Mosquitoland then have the nerve
To claim that this is where the virtuous go
When they die. Watching a line of ants patrol
The counter, she thumbed a few. Without a swerve,
More filled the gap like crumbs of shadow
In a land where sugar hardened in the bowl.

In a land where sugar hardened in the bowl,
It took a while for her to meet the neighbors.
Their languid language always seemed to blur
Like the boiled sugar they poured thick as a drawl
Over pecans to make pralines. *The sole*
Invention of the South, Mom would aver,
Worth the effort. She stirred a whiskey sour.
But solitary scold was not a role
She wanted. She and three wives would convene
For bridge. These ladies hated doing laundry, but
The worst was ironing their husbands' underwear.
When Mom laughed at this "joke," they scowled.
                              They're pralines:
A sweet glaze covering a bunch of nuts!
Though playing bridge is more fun than solitaire.

Though playing bridge is more fun than solitaire,
She needed a friend, a fellow "wife from space"
Whose husband worked with my father in the race
To reach the moon. Someone from home to share
Manhattans chased with arch remarks. Her confrere
Was Barbara Sullivan, as Irish of face
And attitude as Mother. *This goddamn place*
Could give a person Spanish moss for hair,
Said Barbara one day they lunched at the French Market.
That's what drinking from the Mississippi
Can do to you. Mom raised her glass: *Which is why*
God gave us these. Smoking their cigarettes,
They blew rings—twisting mirrors where they could see
The days ahead lay sodden as the sky.

The days ahead lay sodden as the sky
When the doctor said she was pregnant. *I don't need
Another*, she told my father. *We have to feed
Our four; that's enough to satisfy
Me for life.* She shook her head: *I'm much too wise
To be some white trash mom having kids like weeds.*
Though using birth control, my folks had agreed
They still were good Catholics. Was that a lie
She now was being punished for? Dad kissed
And held her—*We'll do whatever you want.*
She seemed to melt into him, fingers pale
From gripping his shoulders. It was the closest
I'd seen them since we came here. A cruel taunt,
The doctor called her pregnancy *abnormal*.

The doctor called her pregnancy *abnormal*,
And she feared deformity. He should have said
The egg had lodged in her tube. A scent of dread
Came through her anesthesia like a gale
Only she could smell. Would the marriage fail?
Back from the knife, mysteries she hadn't read
Lay unopened. A damsel in distress fled
The house across the street, asking Dad to nail
Some loose shingles on her roof. Vietnam
Had called her own man away. *That bitch*,
My mother seethed. I'd never heard her say
The word before. Rising wind brushed the palms.
Dad swayed on the roof at a dangerous pitch.
She shivered, thinking: *Is this the time to pray?*

She shivered, thinking: *Is this the time to pray?*
Despite her clutching the phone tight,
It shook as if cold. She needed to catch a flight
Back home—her mother was whirling away.
When Mom flew off, rain started to streak the clay
Red. Hurricane Betsy flailed its night
Ashore. What were those flashing blue lights?
Cop cars? Transformers blowing. We had to stay
With the Sullivans after the storm passed.
Returning, my mother found her house had drowned,
Fish strewn across the yard. She made a vow:
Once we've left, I'll never come back. Would the blast
Of Katrina cheer her, sinking that steamy ground?
The place we lived is only water now.